CREATING SCENES FOR MILITARY MINIATURES

Groundwork, Foliage, & Settings

Kim Jones

Photography by & text written with Jeffrey B. Snyder

4880 Lower Valley Road, Atglen, PA 19310 USA

I would like to thank Owen Reynolds and Jon Maguire for their fine gallery and cover photography and their ability to work at a moment's notice!

For my wife, Loretta.

Cover photo: "Daddy's Home!". From the collection of Jon Maguire.

Book Design by: Laurie A. Smucker

ISBN: 0-7643-0370-8
Printed in China

Contents

Published by Schiffer Publishing Ltd.
4880 Lower Valley Road
Atglen, PA 19310
Phone: (610) 593-1777; Fax: (610) 593-2002
E-mail: schifferbk@aol.com
Please write for a free catalog.
This book may be purchased from the publisher.
Please include $3.95 for shipping.
Try your bookstore first.

We are interested in hearing from authors with book ideas on related subjects.

Introduction

After you have painted your military miniature you must decide how you are going to display it. You could simply glue it to an attractive base, but you could also create a slice of the actual terrain on which your fellow fought. At this stage a little research is in order so that you have him displayed in the proper terrain and climate. For instance it would be inappropriate to set a British infantryman who fought in the Zulu Wars in a snow setting. Using your reference material, you should be able to determine the types of plants, the lay of the actual land and in some instances the soil color.

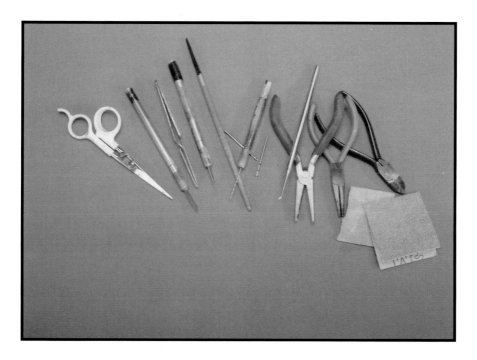

Some of the tools needed for creating scenes. These include scissors, small saw, tweezers, X-acto knife, file, assorted drill bits, plastic scriber, various pliers and side cutters, and assorted grits of sandpaper.

Some of the materials for making foliage. The natural materials you can find in your own backyard or at craft shops that sell dried flowers. You should always be on the look out for nature's props. The items shown here include wild basil, small plant roots, assorted grasses, and small Black-eyed Susans with the petals removed. Surrounding these is a length of jute rope.

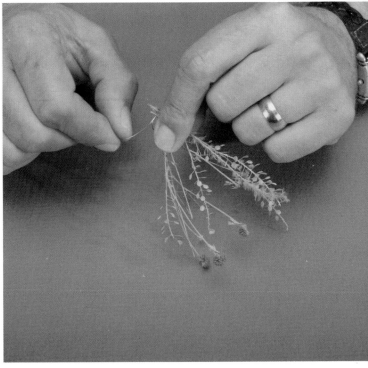

When drying natural plant materials for use in your vignette, you can bind them by the stems with wire or twine and then hang them upside down to dry. This will keep them from falling apart and they will maintain their natural shape.

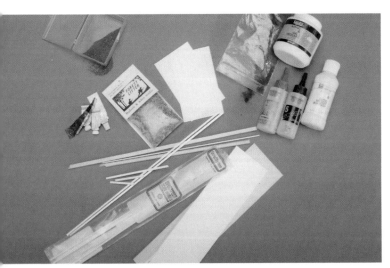

Additional products used to create scenes. These include dried soil sifted through a screen, static grass, acrylic gel medium, wine bottle lead foil, metal foil tubes, forest litter, index cards, five minute Epoxy, gloss acrylic varnish, and assorted sizes of plastic and wood rods and sheets.

Some of the reference books that will give you a good idea of the terrain and foliage. Another good resource would be travel books that can be found at your local library.

Constructing a Bombed Out Building for a World War II Vignette

When constructing scale walls, you must first determine the size according to the scale of the figures you are intending to use in the scene. The materials that you use for wall construction can vary from plastic to wood or even cardboard. The material is not as important as the results achieved. I prefer to use styrene plastic because it is lightweight, easy to cut, and glues together quickly. Here I am laying out the size and shape of the wall that I will construct.

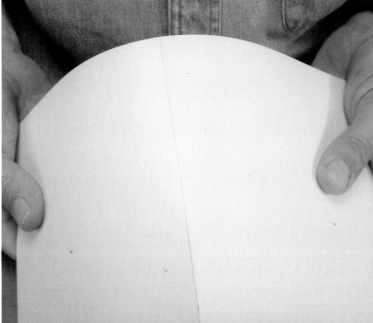

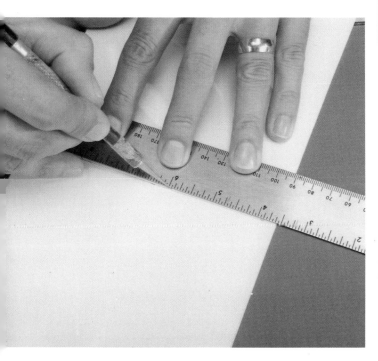

When cutting styrene plastic, simply score one time …

…and then bend it to break at the score line.

Cut two pieces of plastic to the same size, one each for the inside and outside of the wall.

Break away the excess plastic.

Lay out the outline of your wall on one piece of the plastic and cut out along the outline of the wall.

Use the previously cut piece as a template. Trace the outline onto the second piece of plastic and cut it out as well.

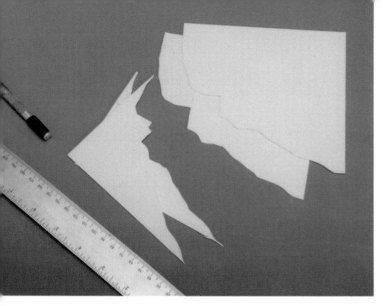

The two pieces of plastic have been cut out. The two halves of the wall are ready for assembly.

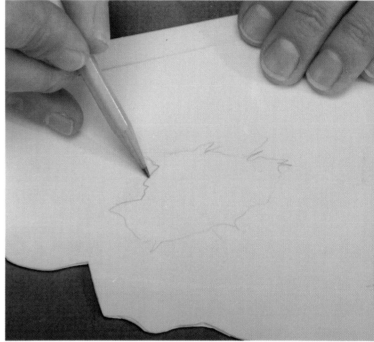

This line indicates an area where the plaster has fallen away from the lath. We will cut this out and fit in the lath later.

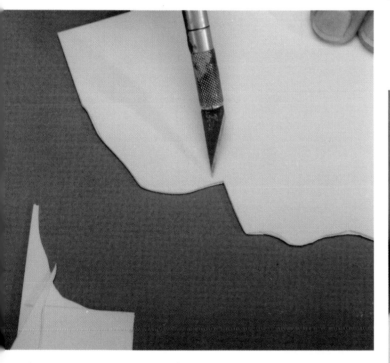

The notch I have indicated in the plastic will be for a window so I can illustrate how to show broken glass.

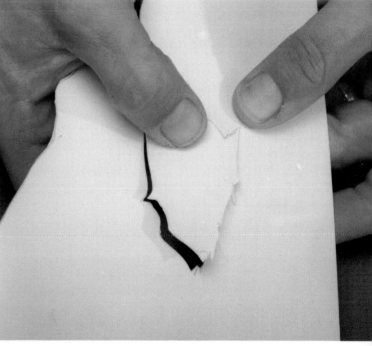

Score the outline with your knife and then begin to work the plastic back and forth until it snaps on the line.

Clean up the edges of your opening with the X-acto knife, following your original outline.

Here I am marking out my stud widths on a piece of basswood of the appropriate thickness. You can purchase pre-sized strips of basswood that would work as well, but I just happened to have this sheet, so I will use it instead. While you could use plastic for the studs, we are using wood because of the effect that it gives when it is broken. It is more in keeping with our ruined building.

Determine the spacing between the studs of your wall and mark them on the plastic. As a rule, studs are generally located on 16" or 24" centers. However, not all studs are set on these standards.

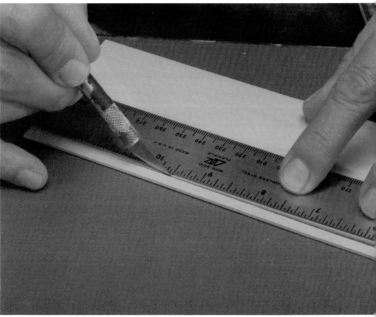

Cut the strips of basswood that will be used for the studs.

Outline the wall panel with the basswood strip. Here I am cutting the basswood to fit the dimension of the wall.

Glue in place along the bottom edge of the wall.

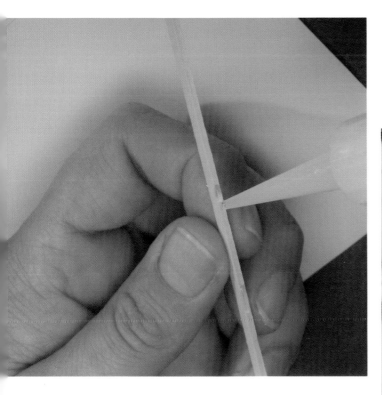

Place a few drops of cyanoacrylate glue along the edge of your basswood.

Continue to size, cut, and glue along the side wall.

9

Determine where the studs go, position the studs, and mark the length, adding about a half inch more than what you need.

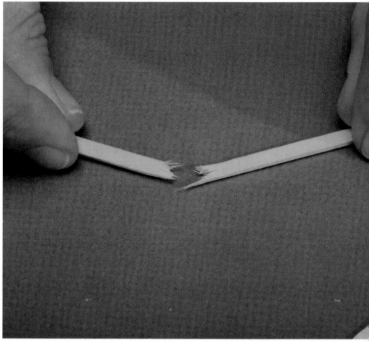

Like so.

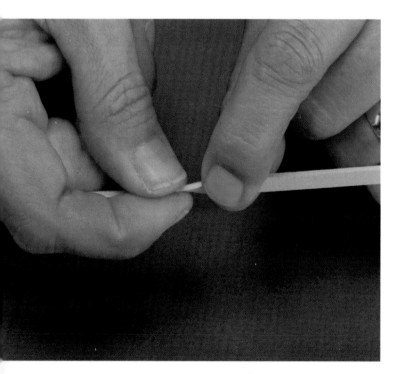

Rather than cutting a straight edge on the stud, twist and break it so that it looks shattered during bombardment.

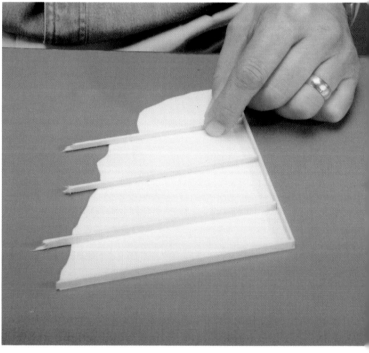

Cut and install all of your studs. If we need to we can come back and further distress the ends of the studs later.

Mark and cut pieces to fit in between the studs.

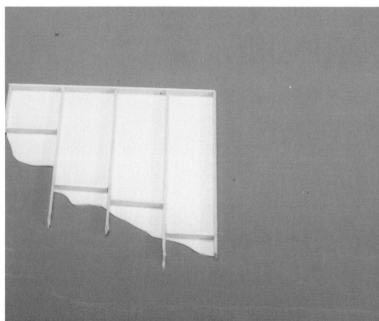

The completed wall interior.

Locate the cross pieces just below the outline of your plastic. This area will be filled with rubble and debris at a later time.

Next, we'll glue on the inner wall covering.

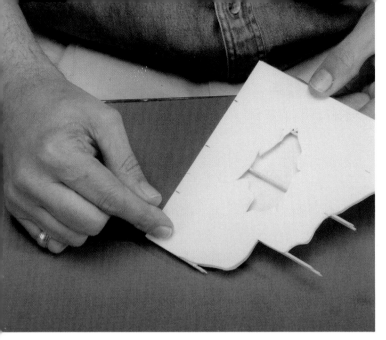

Like so.

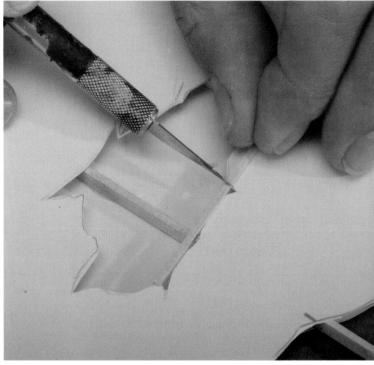

Begin measuring and cutting the strips of wood to fit inside the hole in the plaster.

Cut thin strips that will be used for the lath.

Be sure to cut the ends of your lath to match the outline of the hole.

Cut, fit, and glue the lath in place as you go so that you will have a reference point for cutting the next piece.

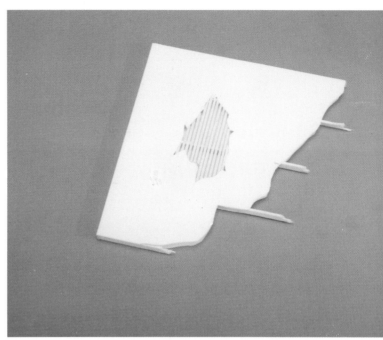

Like so.

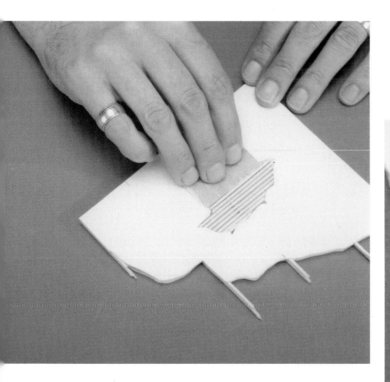

Once the lath is in place, lightly sand to make sure that the lath and surrounding wall are at the same level.

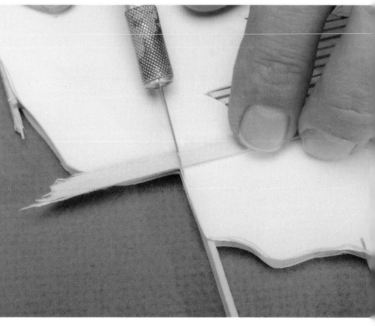

Mark and cut the frame for the window area.

Place the bottom rail of the window frame in place and glue, making sure to keep it at 90 degrees to the stud that it meets.

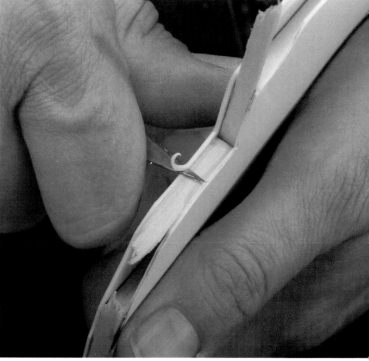

Trim the wall down to meet the window rail.

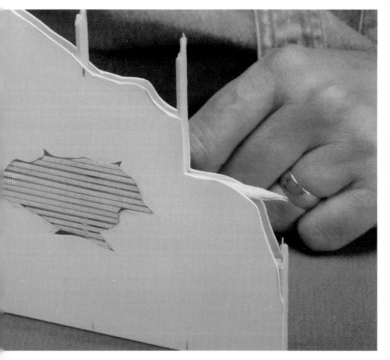

Like so. Notice that we have torn the end of the bottom rail as we did with the studs. Also notice that the wall covering extends above the area of the window rail. We will trim and smooth that next.

The window frame after trimming the wall covering flush.

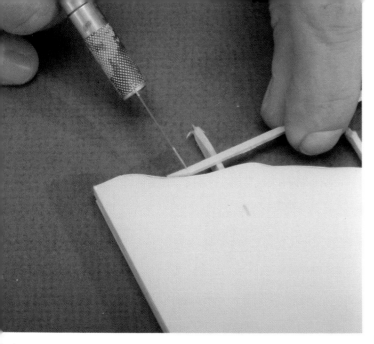

Using the material you used for lath, cut a few and apply them randomly, sticking out horizontally from the side of the wall. We will twist and break the ends of these so that they look ragged as well.

Lightly sand the lath to make sure that it is at the level of the wall covering.

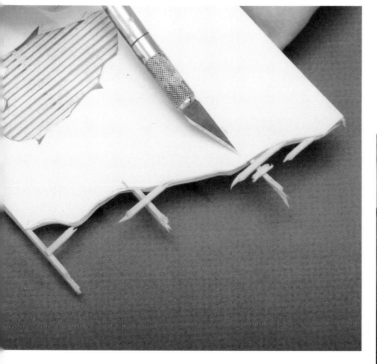

The result.

Using sifted dirt, fill in the areas between the two wall coverings and the studs.

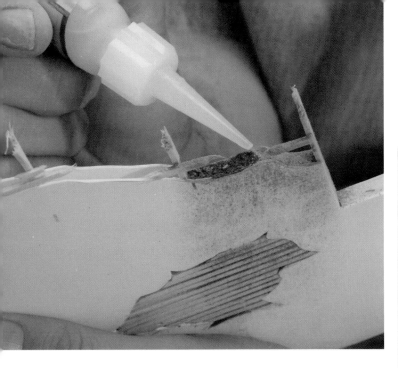

Carefully coat the area with thin cyanoacrylate to solidify it.

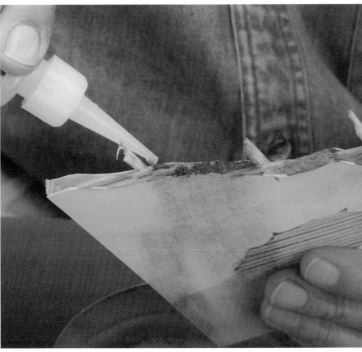

Repeat this process along the rest of the wall.

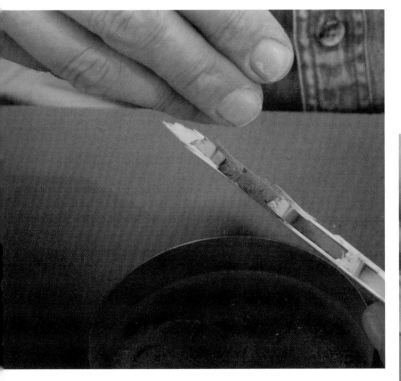

Add more dirt to the top while the glue is wet.

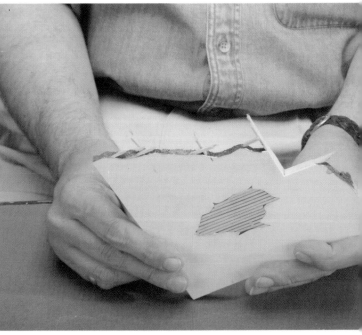

The dirt is now in place.

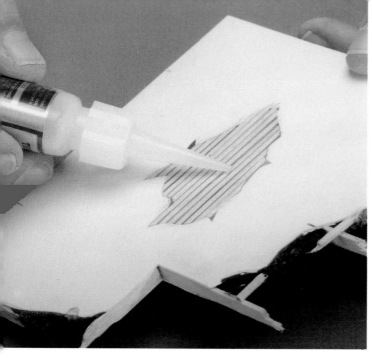

In random areas on the exposed lath, apply cyanoacrylate…

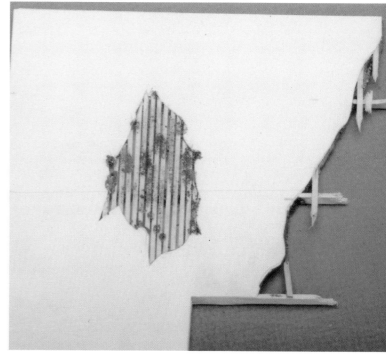

The simulated plaster is in place.

…and gently sprinkle these areas with dirt. This simulates plaster that has remained attached to the lath.

We now turn our attention to the window frame. While in reality after a bombardment this window would not exist, I want to show a pane just to tell you how it is done. Begin by measuring and cutting the lower rail of the window.

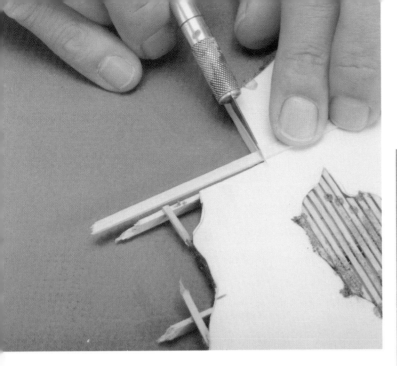

Measure and cut for the side rail. Note that I have torn the top end of the rail.

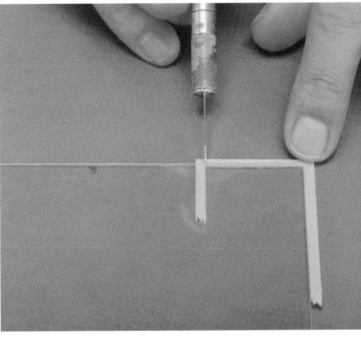

Using a piece of clear styrene mark and cut a piece to fit in the window frame.

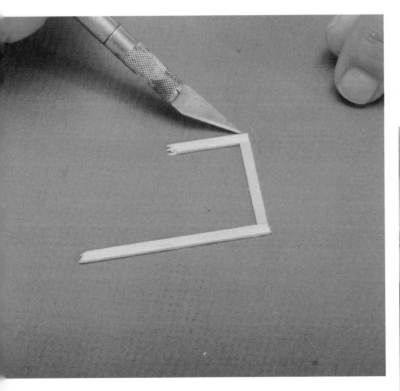

I have cut the other side rail and glued them together.

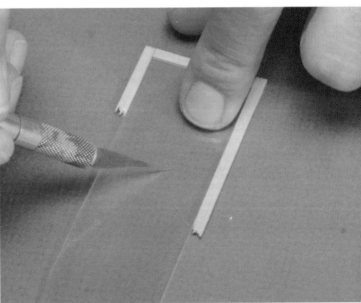

Scribe an outline on the plastic as though it were a shattered pane of glass.

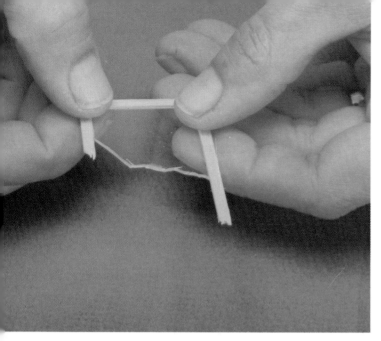

Fit the piece of plastic in place and glue.

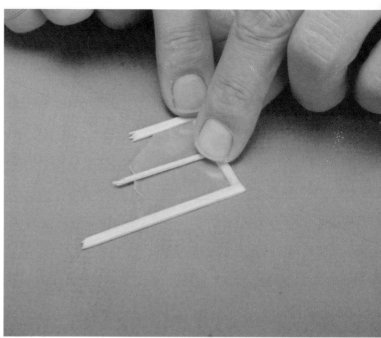

Begin by fitting the middle rail and glue it into place.

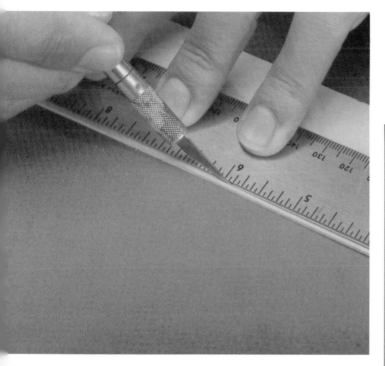

Cut a thin strip of wood. We will use this to separate the individual panes of the window.

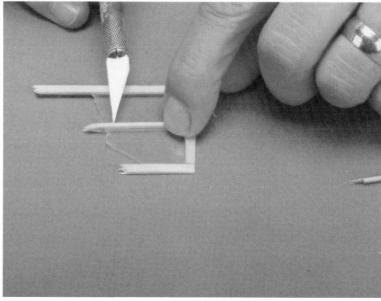

Repeat on the outside of the window.

Measure and cut the cross rails.

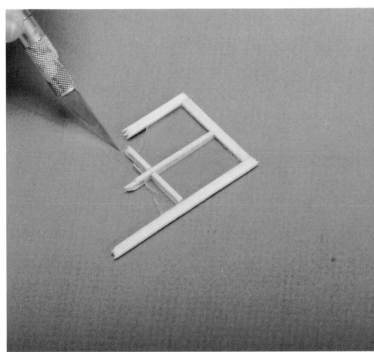

The cross rails are in place.

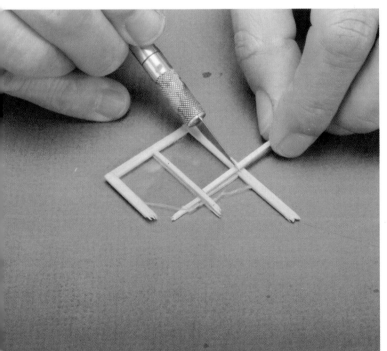

Repeat on the other side.

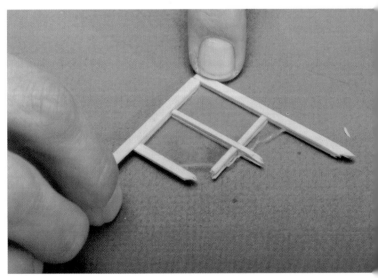

Add additional layers of strip wood to the top and side rails to match the elevation of the window pane rails. Repeat this process on both the inside and outside surfaces.

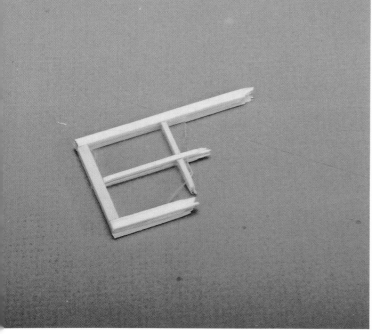

The completed window with all of the rails glued in place.

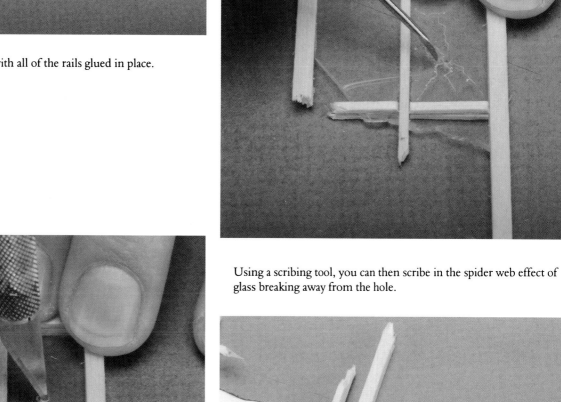

Using a scribing tool, you can then scribe in the spider web effect of glass breaking away from the hole.

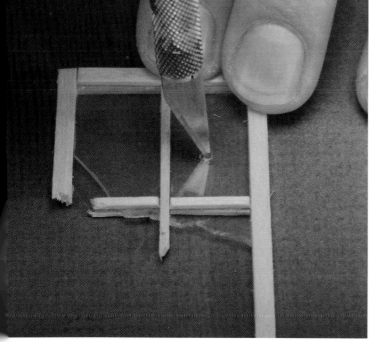

Using the point of your X-acto knife, form a hole in the plastic by repeated twisting. This will create the beginnings of a bullet or fragment hole.

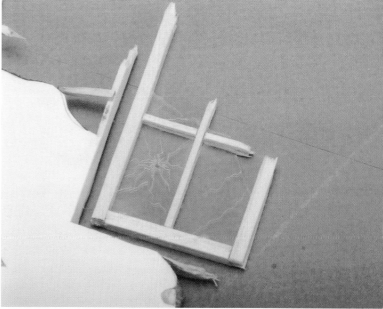

Randomly scribe in lines emanating from the broken top of the window as well. Here is also how the window will eventually fit into place.

Tear off equal amounts of the two parts of A & B Epoxy Putty. We will use this on the outside of the wall to simulate brick and rock.

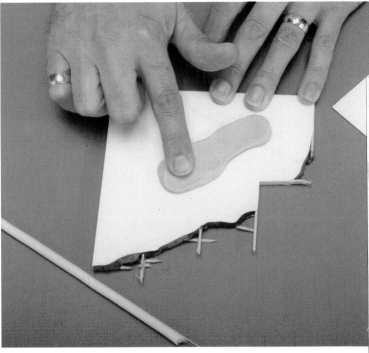

Laying the Epoxy Putty on the outside of the wall. Use your finger to push the putty around evenly on the surface of the wall.

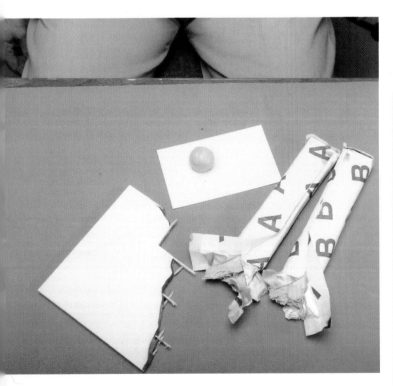

Knead and mix them together thoroughly until the color is uniform.

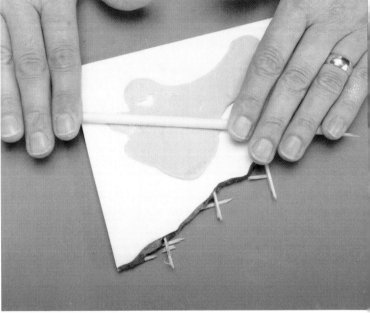

Once you have gotten the putty as thin as you can with your hand you may use a dowel rod to thin the putty further. If the putty sticks to the dowel, dampening the rod with water will help.

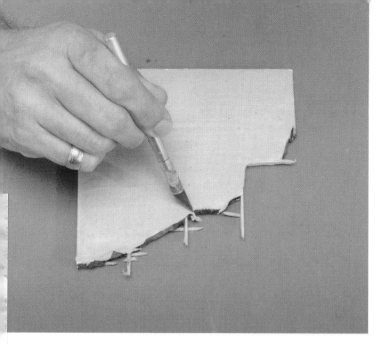

After the Epoxy Putty is spread out evenly, trim off the excess that hangs over the edges.

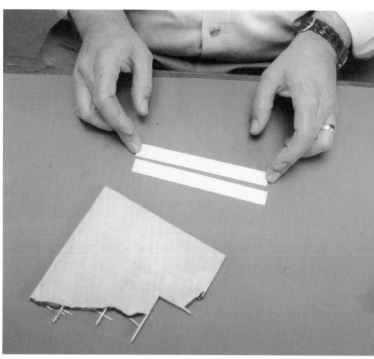

I have cut two pieces of plastic that are longer than the wall's width. These will be used to make a tool for pressing a brick pattern into the Epoxy Putty. These two pieces will be laminated together to add rigidity.

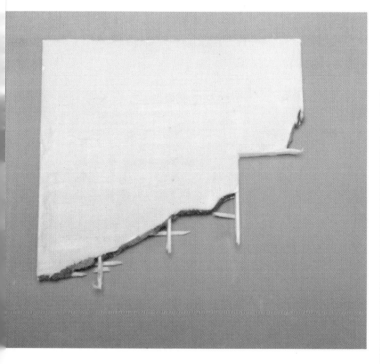

The Epoxy coated wall is ready for texturing.

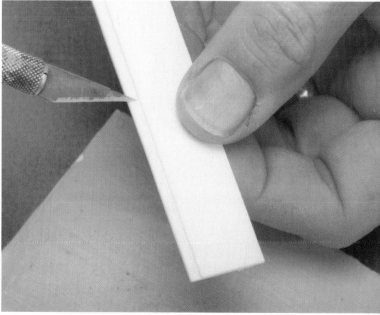

Notice the offset at the edge of the two pieces of plastic. This acts as a stop so we get a consistent depth in the impression we create in the wall.

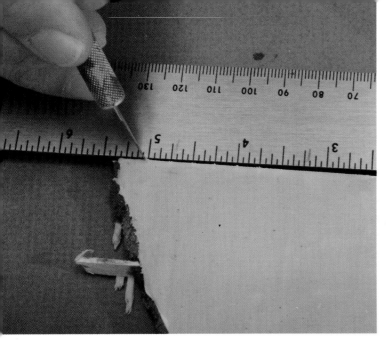

Mark the putty to indicate the height of the bricks and where we will impress the straight edge into the bricks.

Use the tool to create the horizontal mortar lines between the brick courses.

I started my marks 1-1/2" from the bottom. The bottom area will be textured differently.

The end of the tool creates the vertical lines for the first row of bricks.

The second row is offset from the first. Work your way up the wall in the same way.

Add a bit more texture by sprinkling some fine sifted dirt over the wall surface.

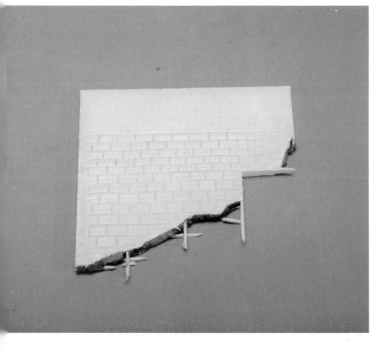

The brick patterning is finished.

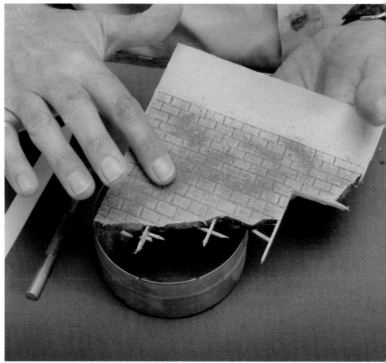

Gently tap the dirt in with your finger and dust off the excess.

Allow the Epoxy Putty to set up until it is almost dry. Then we will further texture and weather the bricks so that they are not so uniform.

After distressing the bricks, add a few bullet holes.

Use an X-acto knife to scrape along the edges of the bricks to make them look weathered.

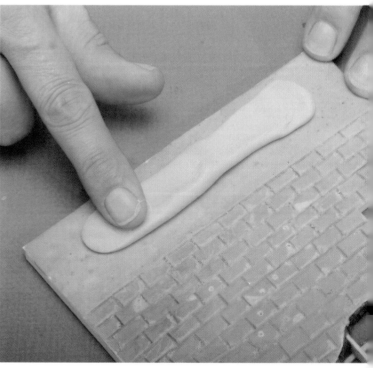

Mix up some more putty. It is time to work on the base of the wall. Spread the putty as before, below the brick line.

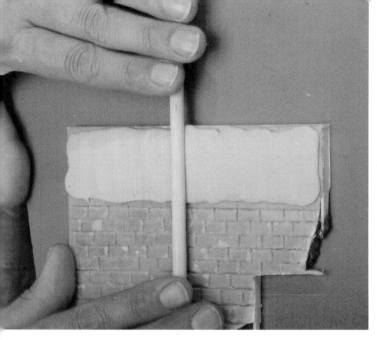

Smooth out the putty with a dowel rod.

You can smooth out the bevel with a moistened finger.

Using the plastic tool constructed earlier, put a beveled edge along the top edge of this lower portion. The bevel acts as a water shed.

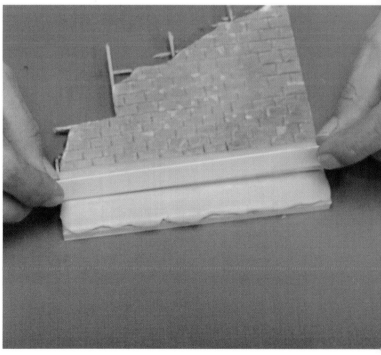

Begin impressing the shapes of large cut stones with the straight edge. Do the horizontal lines first…

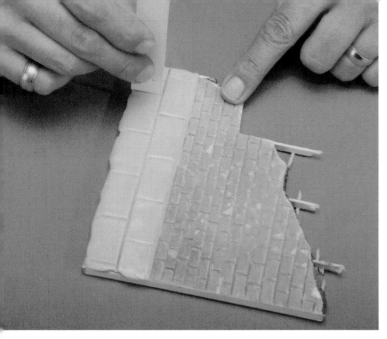

...then add the vertical stone separations.

After the texturing, you may need to use your plastic to redefine the lines between the stones.

Using a stone from the garden, texture the surface of the Epoxy Putty so that it begins to look like cut stone.

Trim the excess putty from around the edges. Then, as you did with the bricks, let the stones dry until they are almost harden. The stone edges will then be textured.

Measure for the window frame. As before, twist and break the ends of the boards.

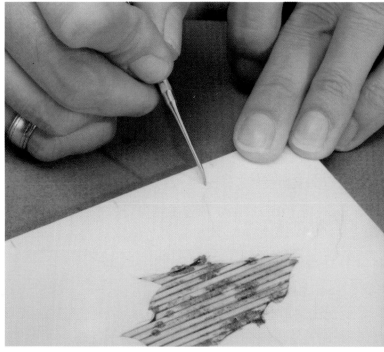

On the inside of the wall, we simply need to add a few cracks to the plaster with the dental probe.

Glue in place with cyanoacrylate.

Use a little bit more dirt and cyanoacrylate to soften the transition between putty and wood.

The transitions have been softened. The finished wall section and window frame—all that is left to do is to determine what position you want the window in, glue it in place, prime the entire piece and paint.

The finished product, primed and ready for painting. A wall like this would make the perfect backdrop for any World War I or II European soldier or any American Civil War figure.

…and inside of the wall.

Here I have attached the wall to a base and glued strips of wood where the wall meets the base to act as filler upon which I will build up the rubble mounds that would have occurred when the wall came tumblin' down. Pile rubble both inside and outside of the wall as you add detail.

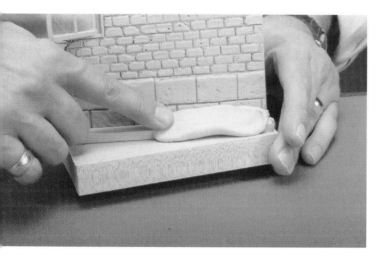

Work Epoxy Putty up to the building and down to the edge of the base to begin to form the rubble mounds. It is not necessary to take too much care as there will be things over this filler.

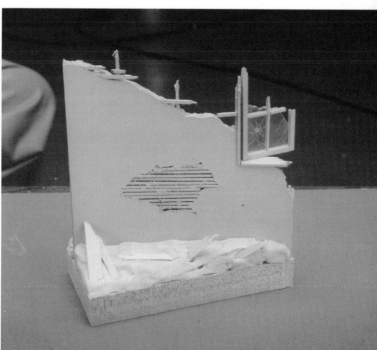

Add randomly torn strips of wood to the wet Epoxy Putty as debris.

The putty base in place on the outside…

Apply chunks of broken Plaster of Paris to simulate large fragments of brick and mortar.

…and then carefully apply cyanoacrylate glue.

Over the rubble you can sprinkle on sifted dirt…

Apply more dirt on top of the glue. Continue moving down the piece, gluing and covering as you go.

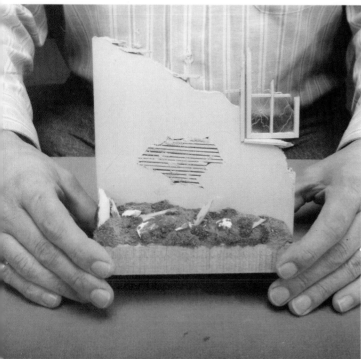

All of the groundwork is now in place. You may vary the level of the groundwork to suit your purposes. Obviously, when a building caves in there is an enormous amount of rubble.

The completed wall and rubble mounds primed and ready for paint.

Creating Foliage

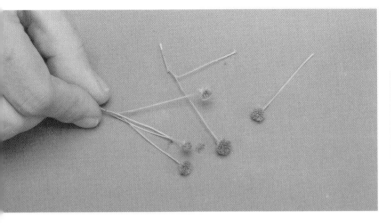

It might be a bit presumptuous to say we are "creating foliage" considering that Mother Nature has actually created it, but we can take many plants from the garden or backyard and modify them to suit our purposes. When possible try to use something natural that in the scale of the model will resemble the plant you want it to be. To begin with, I will make some small cactus-type plants. These are the centers of a small wild flower commonly known as Black-eyed Susans. I remove the petals from around the flower. When dried, these are very fragile, so care must be taken until we can strengthen them with cyanoacrylate.

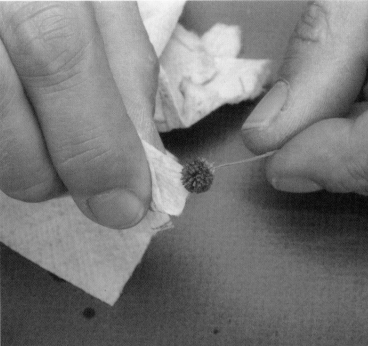

Gently dab the flower with a paper towel to draw off the excess glue. Allow the flower to dry for a short period of time. Prepare several flowers in this manner. Once you have a few of these coated with glue, you can then begin to glue several together.

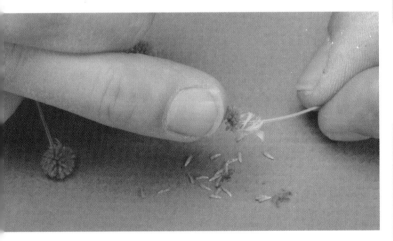

Notice how they fall apart with the slightest touch.

Using the thin cyanoacrylate, coat the plant liberally so that the glue enters all of the cracks and crevices.

The finished bundle of cactus plants.

Set the cacti aside for now. We will combine them with other plants later to show how they will look together. Now we will create a yucca plant from an index card and dried basil.

The exact width is not important as long as none are the same.

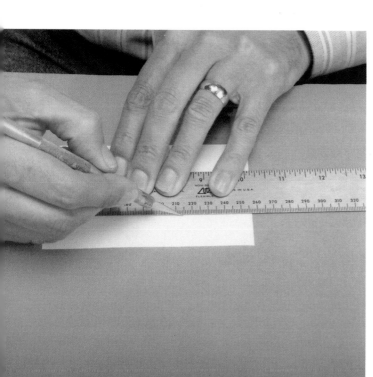

Begin by cutting the index card into three pieces length-wise, and varying widths.

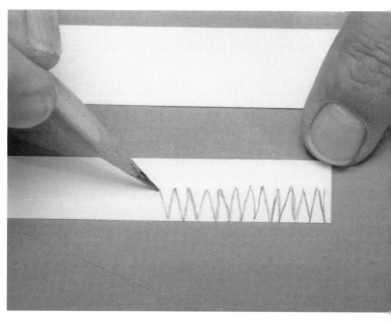

Mark the strips of paper with a pointed leaf pattern. The bottom of the leaves do not go further than half way across the strip of paper. Do this to each of the three strips and then cut them out.

The finished strips of index card after cutting out the yucca leaf shapes.

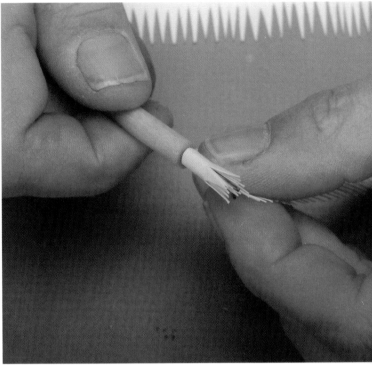

Using the narrowest of the three strips, begin to wind it around the tool.

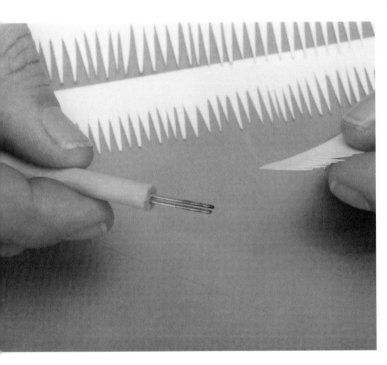

I have constructed a tool to help me make the yucca plant. I have inserted two steel pins cut from a paper clip into a dowel rod. This acts as a take up reel in helping me to wind the index card.

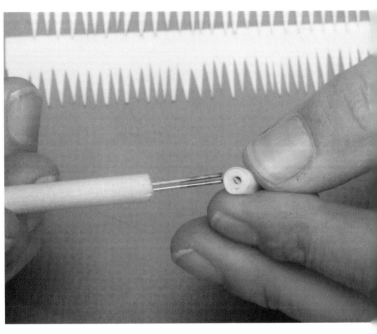

Remove the first roll from the tool and glue it at the bottom with cyanoacrylate.

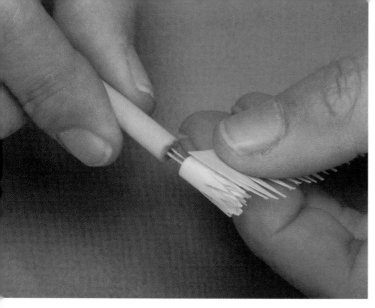

Once the glue is dry, reinsert the tool and glue the second widest length of index card to the one previously rolled and glued.

This is how the three pieces of index card look when they are fully rolled around each other.

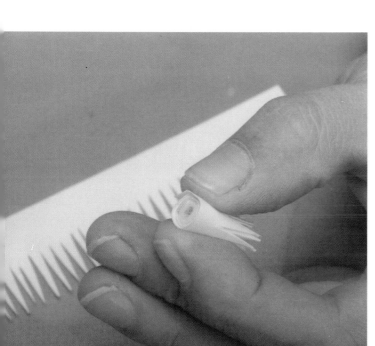

Once the second strip is wound around the first, remove it from the tool and glue the bottom as you did with the first strip. Repeat this process on the widest strip of index card.

Begin fanning the yucca leaves outward, starting with the outermost leaves and working inward.

Continue to unfold the leaves.

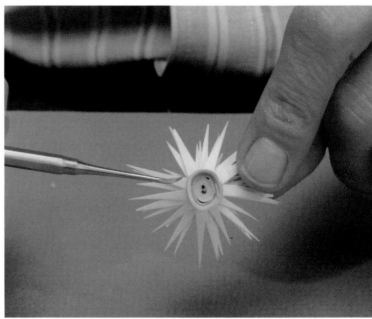

When you are finished wrapping the index card around each other, you will wind up with a large plug under the plant. You can either drill out a hole in the base and use this as a mounting plug or simply cut it off at the base of the plant. If you cut, be careful not to cut too high or the leaves will separate and fall off. I have drilled out the base and use it as a handle to finish the construction and painting of the plant.

The finished plant.

Take the dried basil, feed it through the middle of the index card plant from the top, and glue in place.

Trim off the excess basil stem. This method of creating plants is good for jungle foliage and various reedy plants including cattails and bamboo.

The yucca plant is finished and ready to paint.

Remove some of the seed pods at the bottom of the stem. On the yucca, seed pods are all at the top of the shoot.

To illustrate how the various plants and ground work all work together, I will use this sample block to show various foliage effects. I'll begin as before by spreading Epoxy Putty over the surface of the wood block.

Once the Epoxy Putty is spread, sprinkle on sifted dirt.

You can use real stones and pebbles to create height and improve the visual interest of your base. Set the base aside to dry.

Impress the dirt into the putty.

After priming the yucca plant, glue it to the prepared base with white glue.

Mix a little water with white glue. Apply the watered glue mixture to the base in a random pattern, leaving areas of the soil showing through.

The base is covered with static grass.

Using a product known as "static grass", sprinkle liberally on areas covered in glue. The colors of static grass are usually pretty garish, therefore you should always paint the grass and groundwork.

Blow off the excess static grass. The blowing action causes the pieces of static grass left behind to stand upright. This way it better simulates real grass.

Glue on the small cactus made earlier.

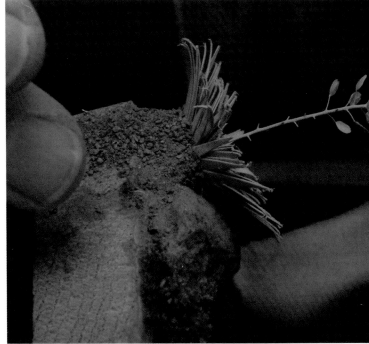

Continue building up the dirt around the yucca plant with alternating layers of dirt and thin glue.

Using sifted dirt and thin cyanoacrylate glue, hide the base of the scene around the yucca plant.

Continue filling the area until it suits you.

Next we'll apply short tufts of jute rope to simulate tall grass. Cut off the length that you desire, holding the rope tightly at the base.

Dip the end in white glue.

Apply the jute rope to the base. Continue in this manner until you cover the area in which you want the longer grass to appear. Don't be too concerned at this point about keeping it too neat. We will trim and arrange the tall grass later so that it looks a little more natural.

Progress.

The rope now has a much more natural look. Set aside to dry. If you have a large area to cover with the taller grass, do it in sections about this size so that you can set it and stir it before the glue hardens too much.

Once the glue is set, use a pointed object (such as your plastic scriber) to separate the various strands of rope. Use almost a stirring action to create a random, natural appearance.

Trim the tops of the tall grasses with a random pattern to create a more natural look.

Cut grass.

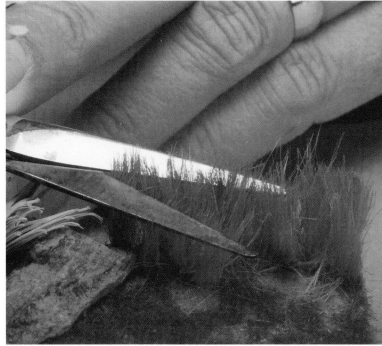

…rather than straight across the top. This will give the grass a more varied appearance, rather like a bad haircut.

Try to use the points of your scissors in a downward motion…

At this point your base is ready to paint. Remember when painting groundwork you should paint everything, even the natural plants that you may have used. You will want to use the same weathering techniques on your plants that you used on your figure.

45

Making a Folding Camp Chair

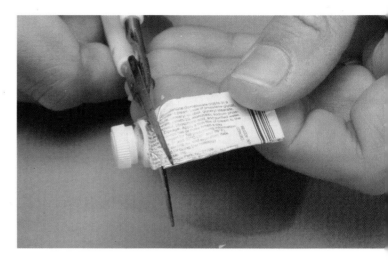

Prepare metal tube for use by cutting the spout off. Discard the spout.

Most of the figures and scenes I create depict soldiers in their off-duty time such as in garrison or camp life. In studying some of the old photographs of nineteenth century military life you will find the ubiquitous folding camp chair. This type of chair was used by every military power of the period.

Unwind the tube.

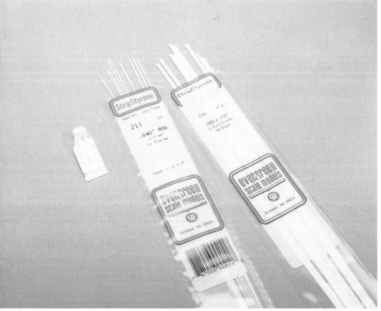

These are the materials we will use to construct our camp chair. Left to right: an empty metal medicine tube, .040 styrene rod, .060 x .100 styrene strips. These are the sizes I use as I work in 120mm figures. You need to use whatever size suits your purpose. We'll construct the framework from the plastic and the carpet seat from the metal tube.

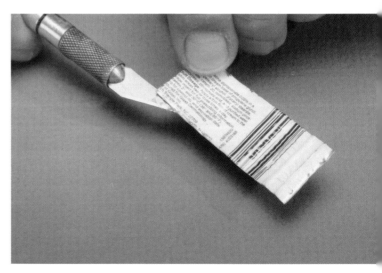

Cut open one side of the tube. Be careful not to cut yourself or pierce the side of the tube. Clean out the tube with dishwashing liquid and water.

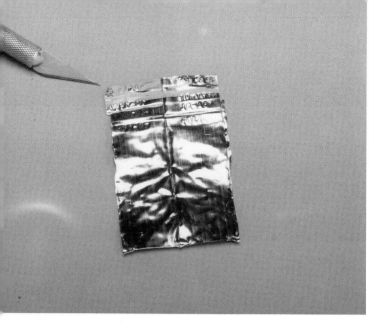

This is what you are left with.

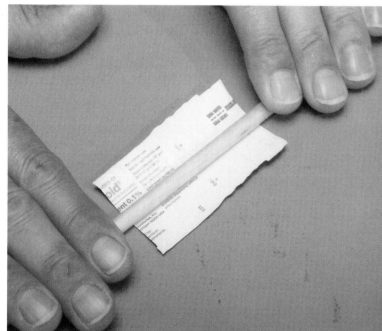

Roll from both sides and in all four directions.

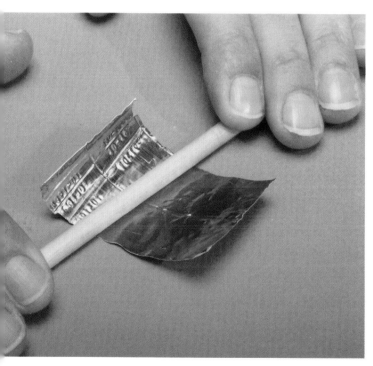

Using a piece of dowel, roll the piece of metal flat.

Cut away the section of the tube that has embossed numbers. They simply can't be rolled away.

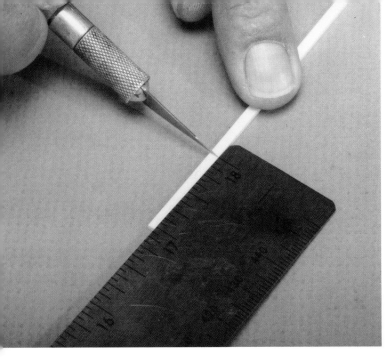

For this chair we'll begin with the back by cutting two one inch lengths of the strip styrene.

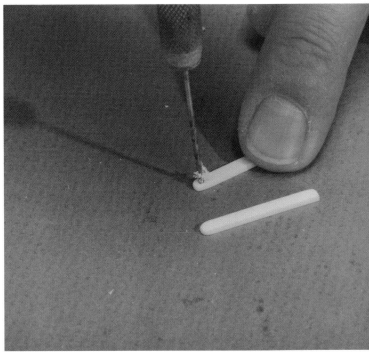

Using a pin vice and a drill bit the same size as your plastic rod, drill through the bottom of the rail.

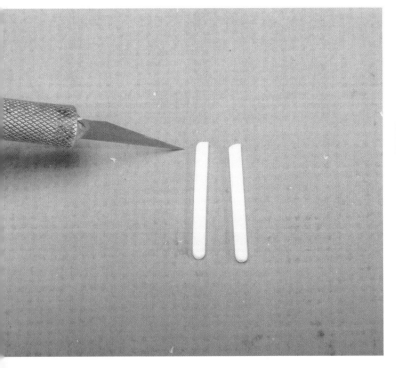

Round off both corners of the bottom of the rail with sandpaper but only one corner of the top.

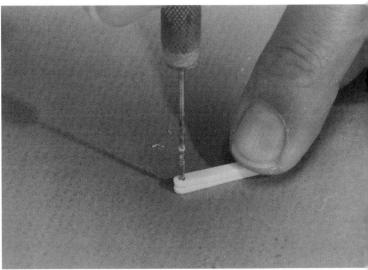

To be sure that the holes in both rails line up, put them together and drill through both, using the hole in the previously drilled rail as your guide.

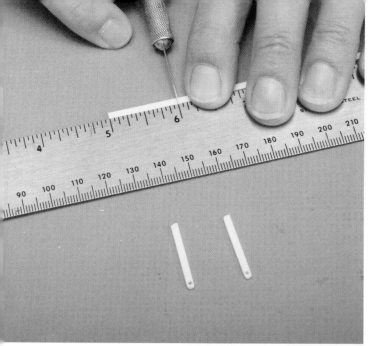

Cut three more one inch pieces that will serve as the back rails.

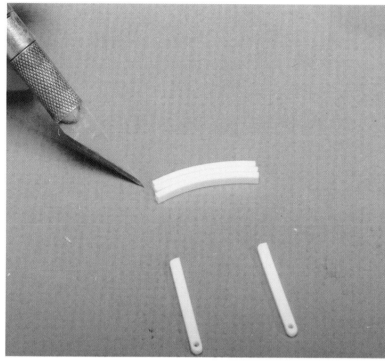

…like so.

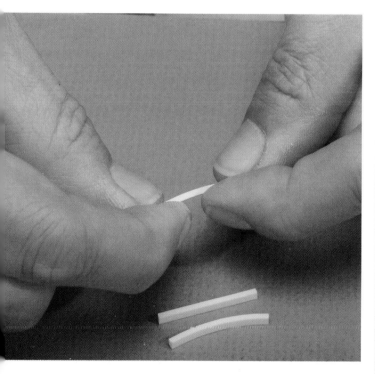

The back rails should have a slight curvature to them. This is achieved by bending them with either your fingers or the dowel rod. The important thing is that all three have the same curve…

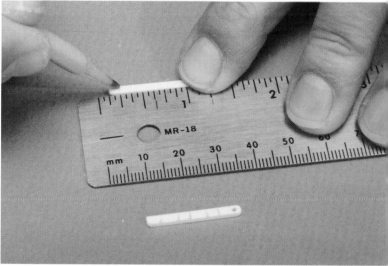

Marking the spots where the rungs of the back of the chair will be attached.

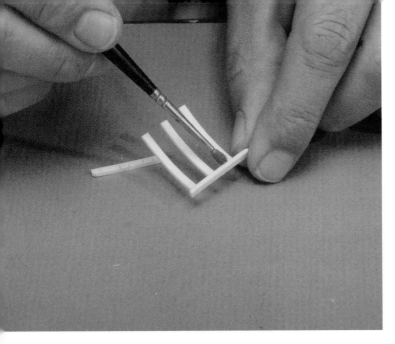

Glue the rungs of the chair back to one side rail. Use a water thin glue made for acrylic for this. It makes a very strong bond and melts the plastic together. It is also quick drying. The acrylic glue is also much stronger than cyanoacrylate would be when it comes to placing a figure in the chair.

The completed chair back.

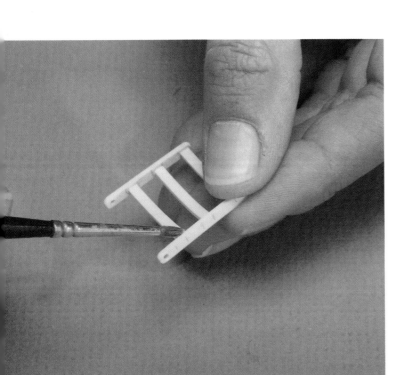

Glue the other back rail to the slats.

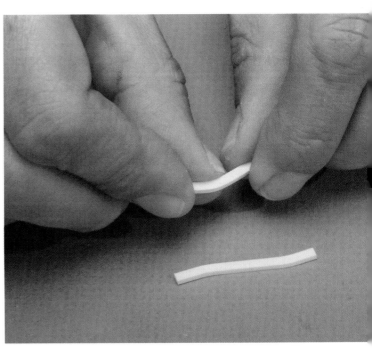

Moving on to the camp chair legs and seat. Putting a slight S bend to the legs. Don't worry about the length right now. The length between the two curves must be the same at this point. We will trim the legs later. Make two sets of these legs.

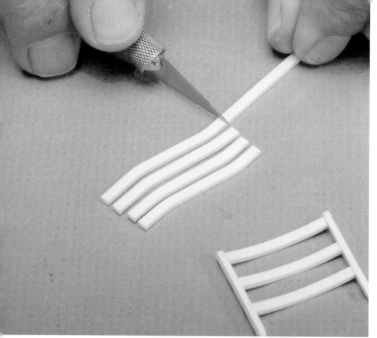

Cutting the last leg. Note that the S curves all match up.

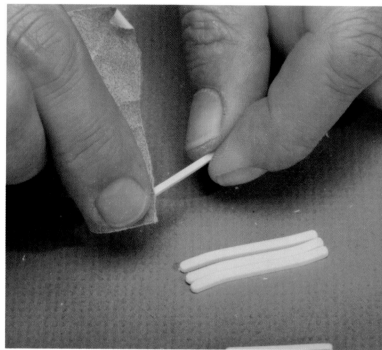

Round off the corners at the end of each leg.

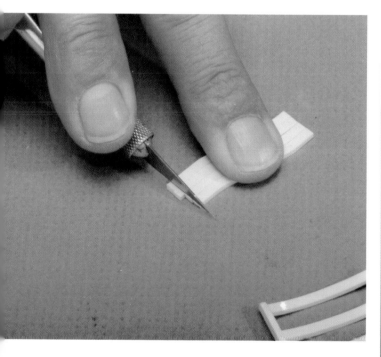

Trim the length of all of the legs to match.

You can mark the middle of the legs prior to drilling a central hole.

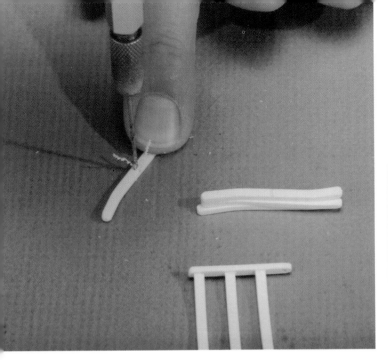

Drill a hole through one and then use it as a guide to ensure that all four will line up later.

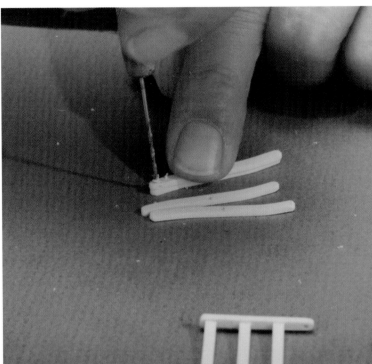

Drill holes in one end of the legs only. Again, drill one leg and then use it as a guide for the other three.

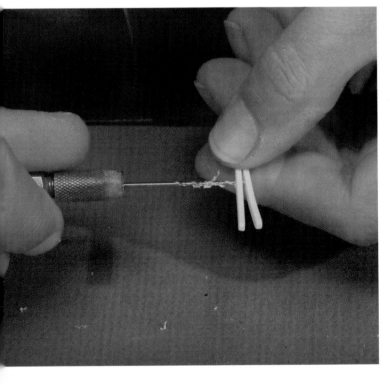

Use the first drilled leg as a guide for the other three legs.

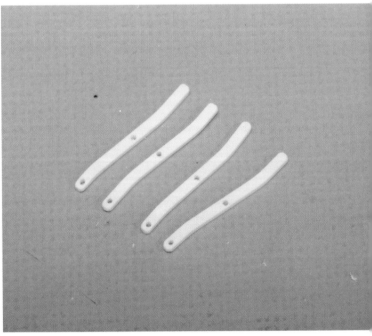

The four legs are drilled and ready for rods.

Cross the legs in this configuration.

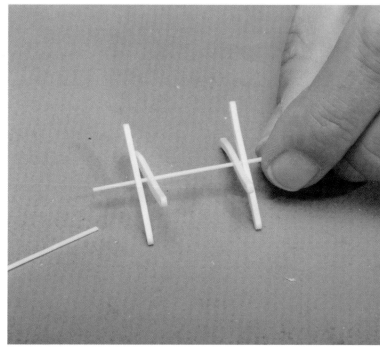

Cut the dowel rod, leaving it longer than will eventually be needed.

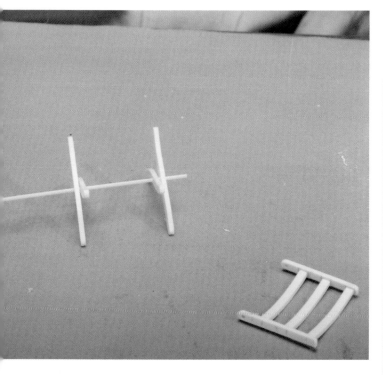

This shows the proper alignment of the rails. The inside rails are the ones that will attach to the back.

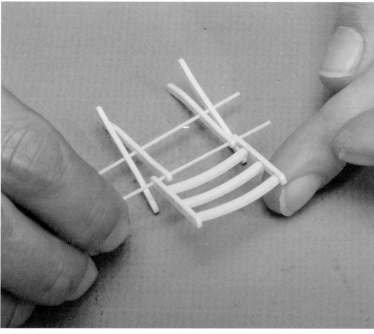

With the legs lined up inside the back rails, thread the rod through the four pieces. Again cut the rod longer than needed.

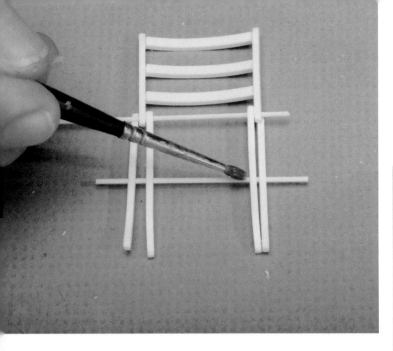

Line up the inside legs where they run parallel to the rails of the back and put a spot of glue at the point where the rod runs through the center of the legs only.

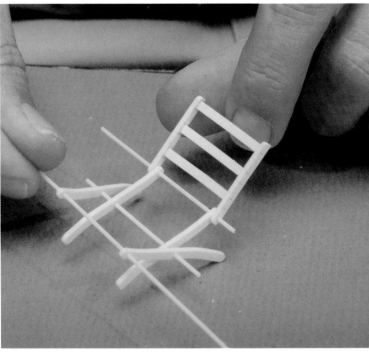

Insert the rod through the forward part of the back legs, the front edge of the seat.

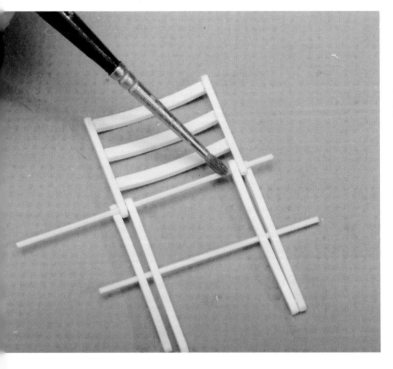

Now put a drop of glue where the rod runs through the top of the legs, at the point where they attach to the back.

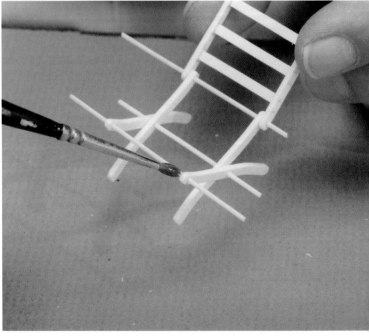

After inserting the rod in the top part of the leg, put a drop of glue along the inside edge of the rail where it meets the dowel.

Now is the time to determine from the figure you are going to put into the chair the distance that you will need in the seat area of the chair...indicated by the two points of the scissors.

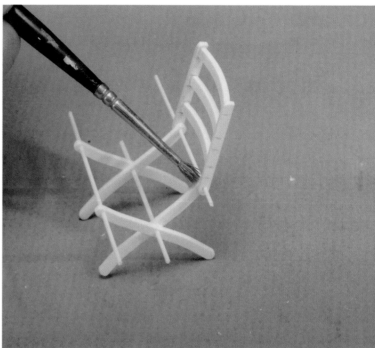

Now determine the angle of the back and glue it at this point and the opposite point. Set aside to dry thoroughly before moving on to the next step.

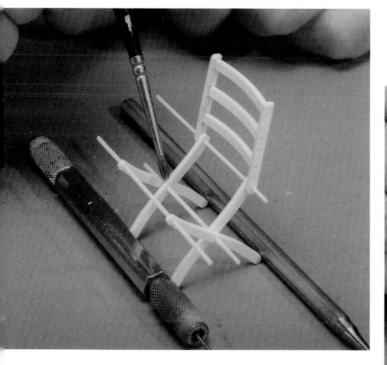

Once that distance is determined, you can hold the chair in position by applying glue at the intersections of the legs.

Once the glue is dried, trim off the excess dowel.

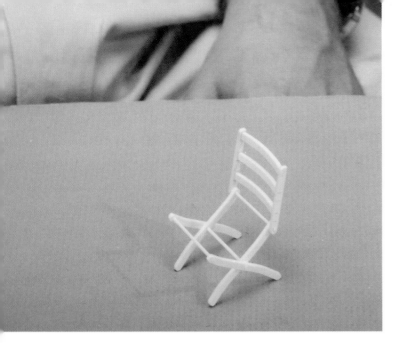

The dowel rods are trimmed. The chair is ready for its seat.

Trim the flattened tube material to width.

After squaring up two sides of the prepared metal tube, mark the width that you will need at the back of the chair.

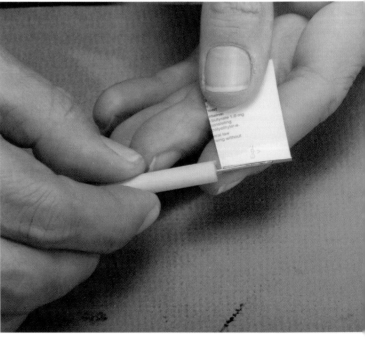

Using the tool we made earlier for winding up the yucca plant, round over the back edge of the seat.

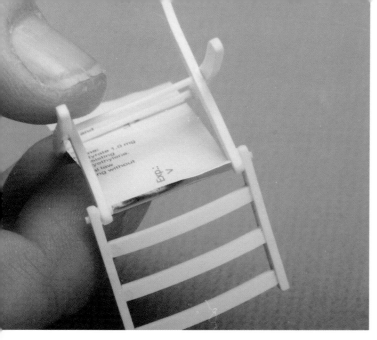

Hook the rounded edge over the back dowel on the seat.

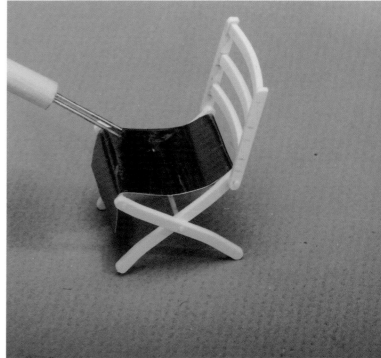

Determine the amount of sag you want in the seat.

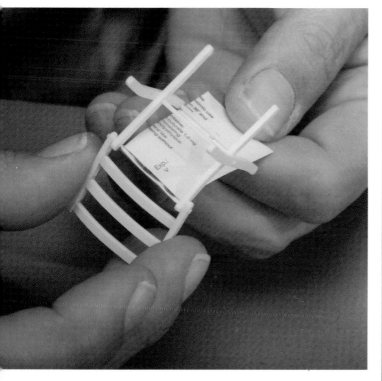

Glue this end in place with cyanoacrylate glue.

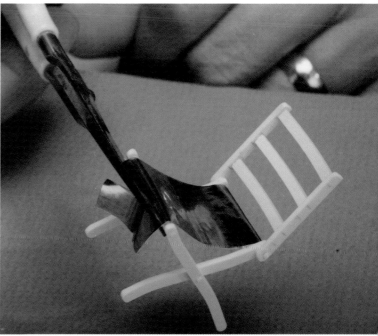

Fold the leading edge of the material over the front dowel rod and trim the excess away with scissors.

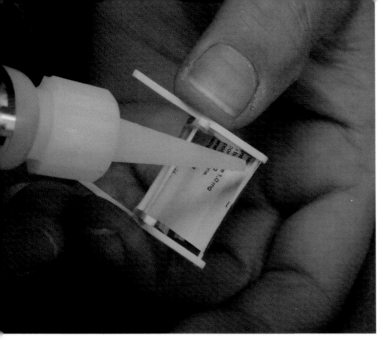

Glue in place from underneath.

The completed chair, ready for primer.

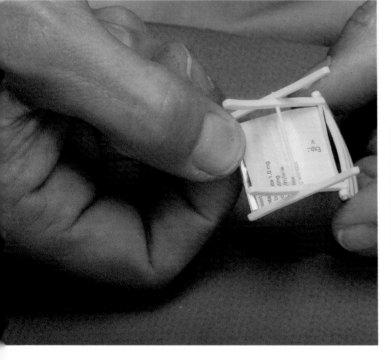

Continue pressing the material around the dowel.

The camp chair is primed and ready for painting.

The Gallery

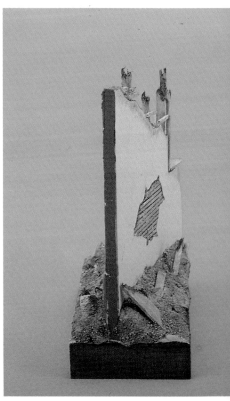

"My Dearest Autie", showing a typical camp chair.

The Prize

Detail of "The Prize" showing cacti made from natural material.

61

Detail showing groundwork and small root emerging from the ledge.

No Beans Tonight!

Detail of "No Beans Tonight!" showing the use of natural grasses to create prairie grass.

A Fearful Noise

Detail of "A Fearful Noise" showing constructed yucca plant and natural rocks to create the scene.

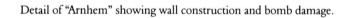

Arnhem. *From the collection of Jeff Hudson.*

Detail of "Arnhem" showing wall construction and bomb damage.

Close-up of broken wall with lath showing.

Honoring the Colors

Close up of "Honoring the Colors" showing a tree trunk made from real twig textured with epoxy putty to simulate bark. The vines are made from lengths of small roots.